Going to the Dentist

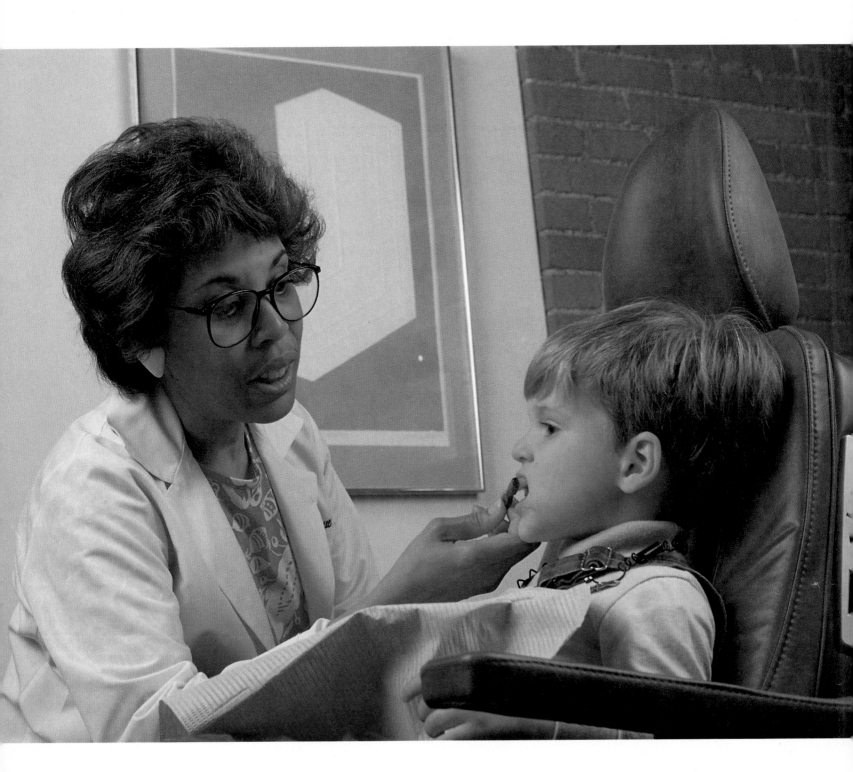

Going to the Dentist

BY FRED ROGERS

photographs by Jim Judkis

G. P. PUTNAM'S SONS
New York

With special thanks to: Nan Earl Newell;
Margaret B. McFarland, Ph.D., Senior Consultant;
the American Academy of Pediatric Dentistry,
Judith M. Davenport, D.M.D.,
Marcus A. Gottlieb, D.D.S., Consultants;
Barry N. Head; the Kelly family; the Kinder family;
and all the other families and friends who
helped us with the book.

Text and photographs copyright © 1989 by Family Communications, Inc.
All rights reserved. Published simultaneously in Canada.
Printed in the United States of America.
Project director: Margy Whitmer
Book design by Kathleen Westray
Library of Congress Cataloging-in-Publication Data
Rogers, Fred. Going to the dentist / by Fred Rogers;
photographs by Jim Judkis. p. cm.
(A Mister Rogers' first experience book)
Summary: Prepares a child for his first visit to
the dentist by describing the procedures, equipment,
and staff involved in a dental examination.
Includes tips on keeping teeth clean.
1. Teeth—Care and hygiene—Juvenile literature.
2. Dentistry—Juvenile literature.   3. Children—
Preparation for dental care—Juvenile literature.
[1. Dental care.   2. Dentistry.   3. Teeth—Care and hygiene.]
I. Judkis, Jim, ill.   II. Title.   III. Series: Rogers, Fred.
Mister Rogers' first experience book.
RK63.R64   1989   617.6 - dc19   88-15045   CIP   AC
ISBN 0-399-21636-7
ISBN 0-399-21634-0 (pbk.)
First impression

Mouths are one of our most important body parts when it comes to our development as human beings. Anything that affects our mouths will have a great effect on us . . . so it's not surprising that going to the dentist for the first time can be a most important step in a child's life.

What may be hardest for children at the dentist is to have to open their mouths and let in the dentist's hands or strange instruments. The less children have mastered their urge to bite, the harder it may be for them to allow such intrusions.

As children struggle to cope with dental procedures, the biggest help will be a trusting relationship with the dentist and the dentist's helpers. Your choosing a dentist who cares about children and their special needs is the best way to begin: If you, as a parent, feel good about a dentist, the chances are your child will more than likely sense your confidence and have positive feelings, too.

It's also a help to time your child's first visit to the dentist well before any problems arise—perhaps even before your child's first birthday. You can consult your own dentist or your child's pediatrician about that. Early visits give your child an opportunity to get to know the dentist, the assistants, the office and the equipment. These can be times without anxiety to begin forming a trusting relationship.

Of course, the foundation for your child's relationship with the dentist lies in open and honest communication between your child and you. That's, in part, why we've made these First Experience books—to help parents and children find their own ways to talk about what's important to them. We trust that you will find this book a helpful springboard for your beginning conversations with your child about going to the dentist.

—FRED ROGERS

Learning to take good care of yourself is an important part of growing. No matter how much you grow, though, there will always be times when you'll need help in keeping your body healthy. That's true for everyone—children and adults.

Moms and dads know many ways to help keep their children healthy. And there are people like dentists and doctors who know things that even most moms and dads don't know.

Dentists know a lot about teeth and how to keep them clean and strong. That's important because you'll need your teeth for eating just about everything that helps you grow.

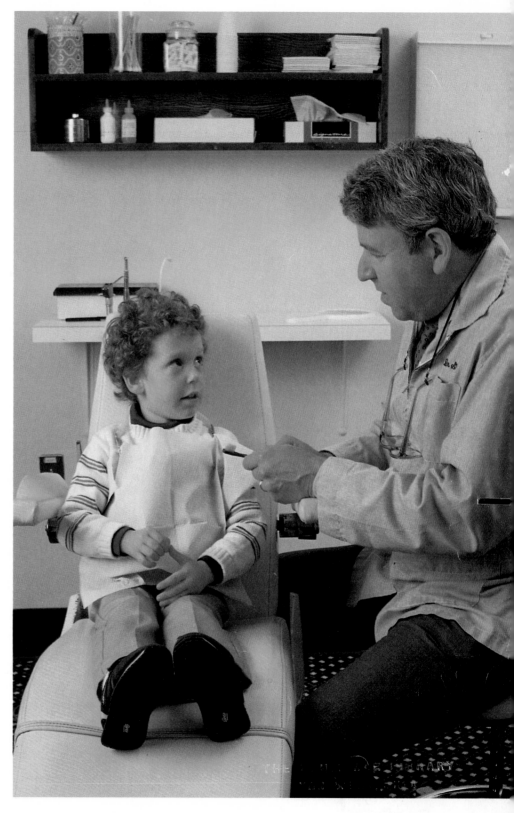

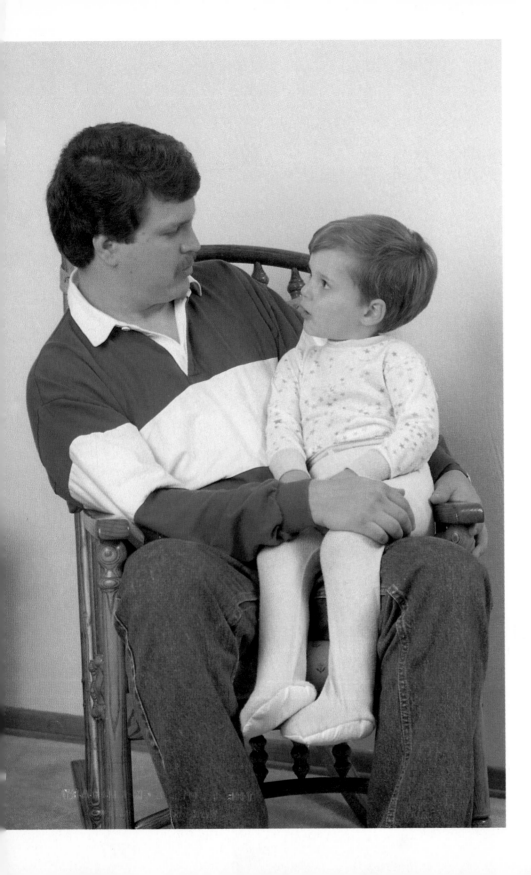

If it's time for you to go to a dentist's office, you may be wondering what it will be like and what the people there will do. You could talk with someone you love about going to the dentist.

You could pretend about it, too.

When you go to the dentist's office, you usually have to wait for a while in the *waiting room*. You'll probably find magazines there and maybe even some toys. You might want to bring a book or toy from home . . . and that's fine.

When it's your turn, you'll go into another room. If it's your first visit, you might want the grownup who's with you to keep you company. Many dentists understand that children can find it hard to do something the first time all by themselves.

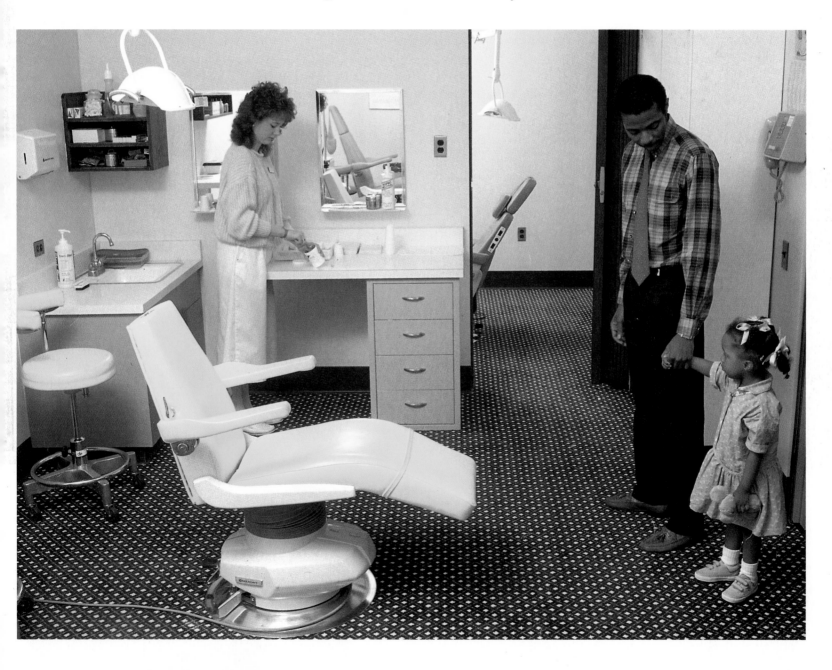

The first person who looks at your teeth may be one of the dentist's helpers, and that person is usually a woman.

She'll be the one to make sure you get settled comfortably in the big *chair* that goes up and down. If you ask her, she might show you how it works.

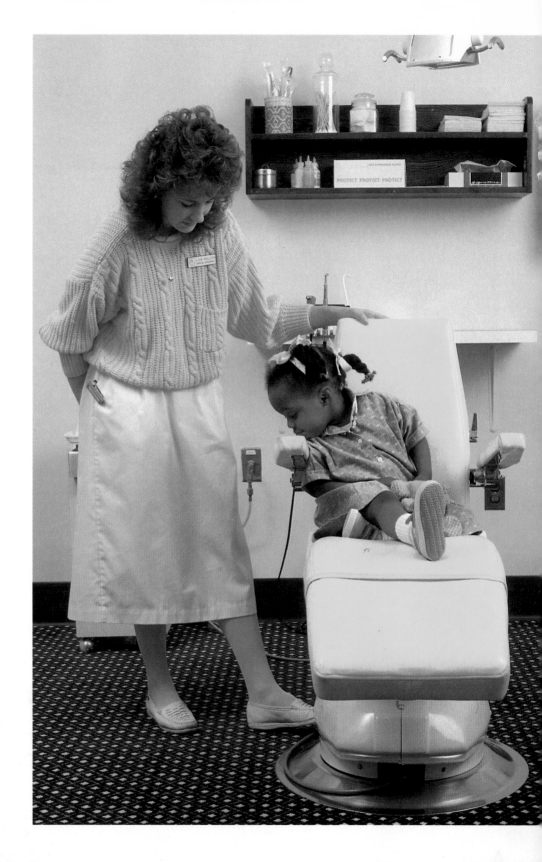

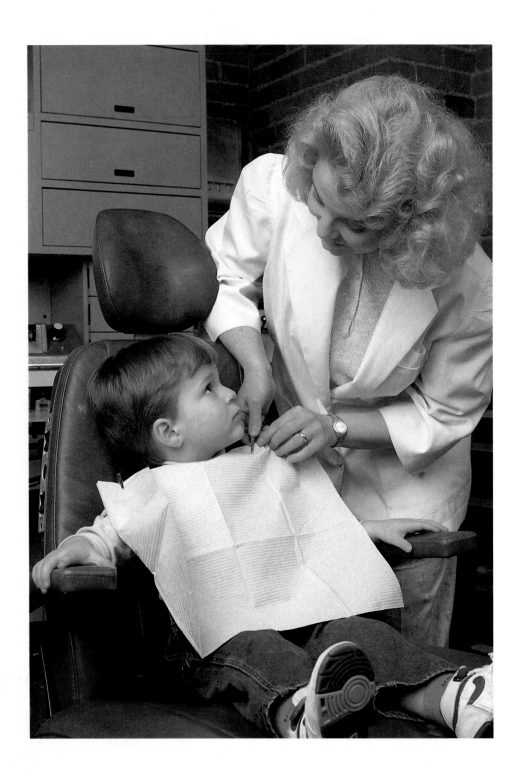

Then she'll probably clip a *bib* around your neck to keep your clothes clean and dry. Everyone who goes to the dentist wears a bib—even grownups!

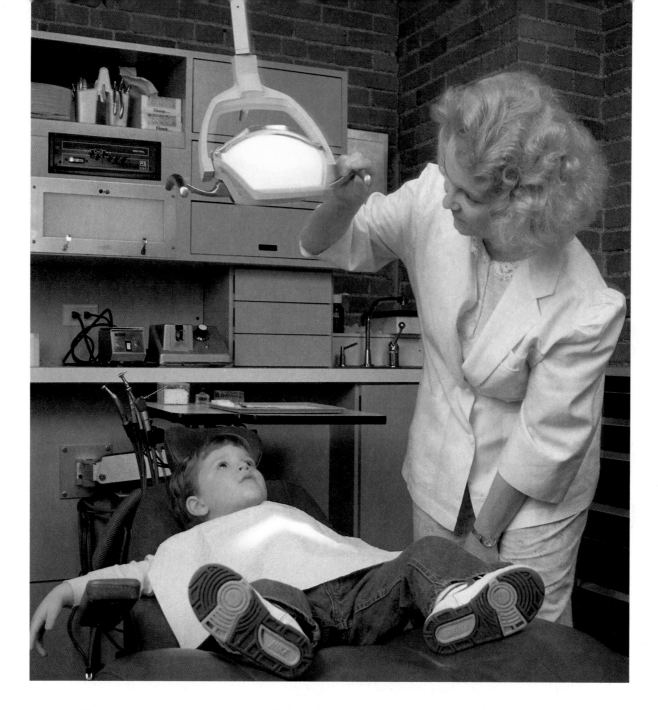

She might turn on a big, bright *light* above your head
and move it around so it shines into your mouth . . .
but not into your eyes.

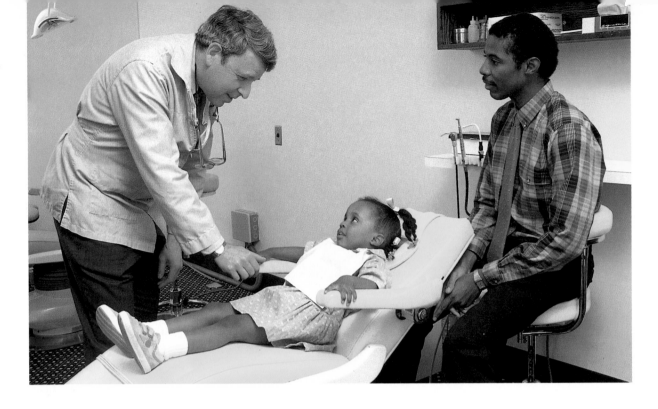

Soon you'll meet the dentist. The dentist can be a man or a woman. Do you know which your dentist will be?

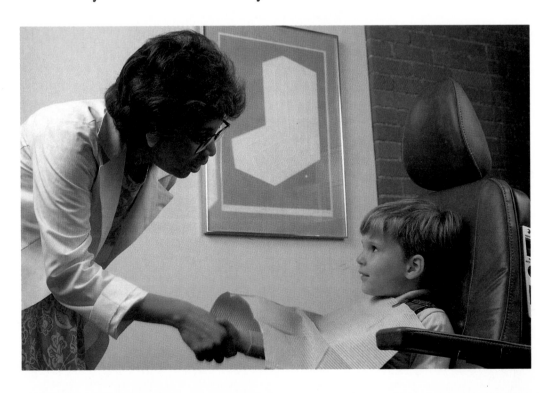

Dentists and their
helpers usually
wear gloves when
they're checking
your teeth. That
way, your mouth
can stay clean, and
so can their hands.

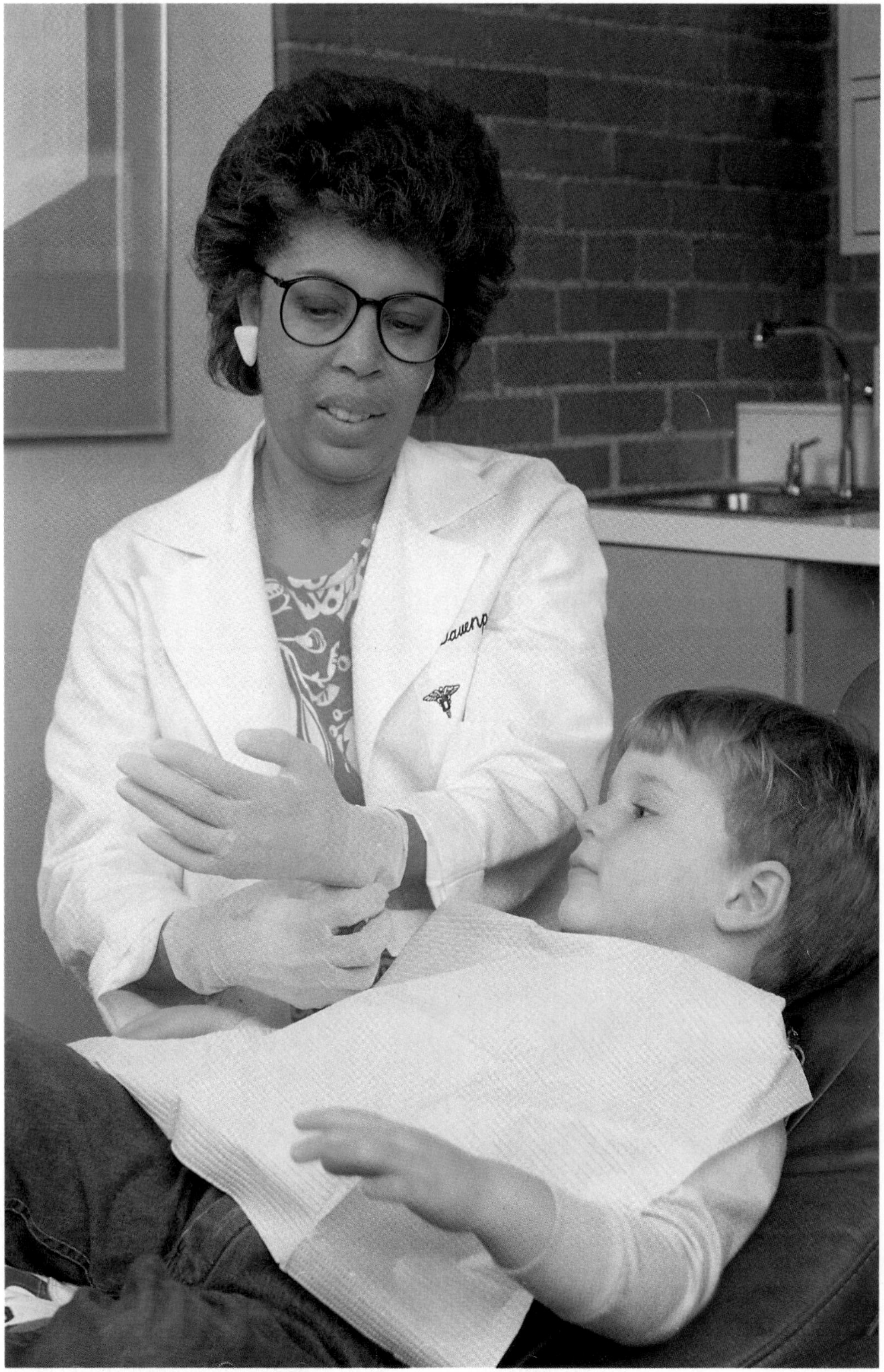

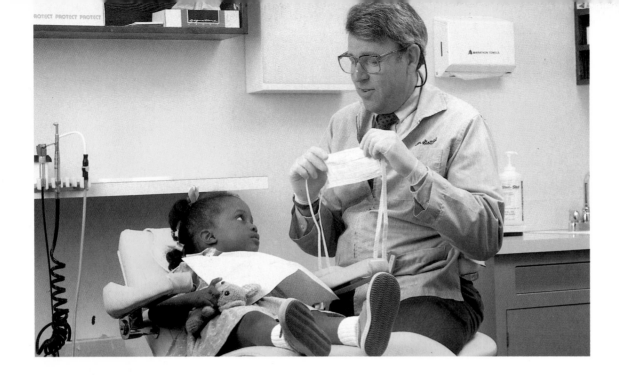

They may wear masks, too. That's to protect you both from germs. Under their masks, dentists and their helpers are still the same people—people who want to take good care of you!

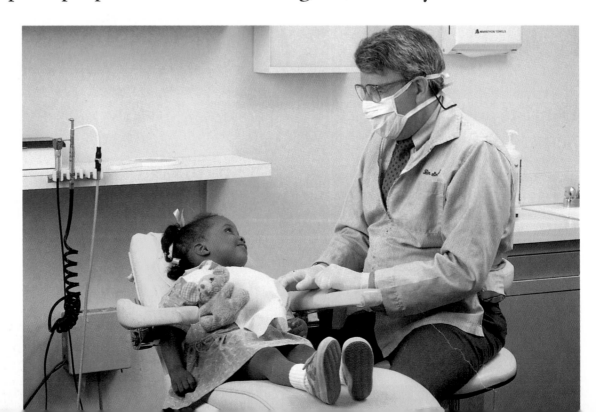

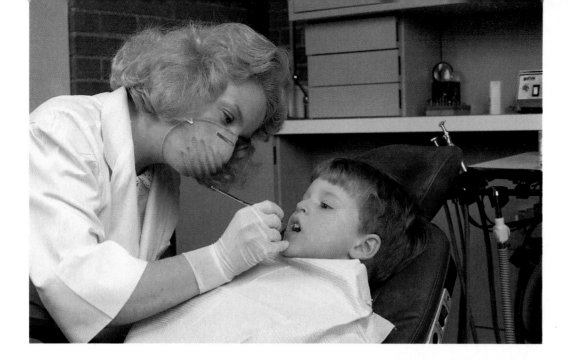

Dentists and their helpers
have special tools that they
know how to use in their
work:

• an *explorer* to count your
teeth and clean out the places
between them;

• a *mirror* to help them see
behind your teeth and all
around your mouth;

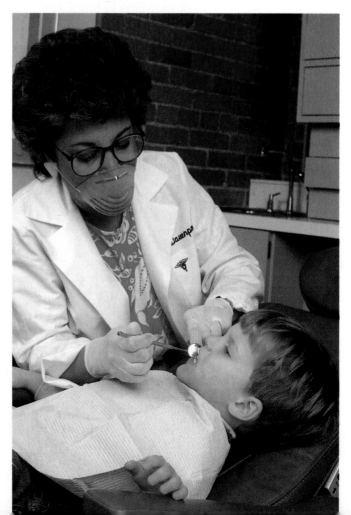

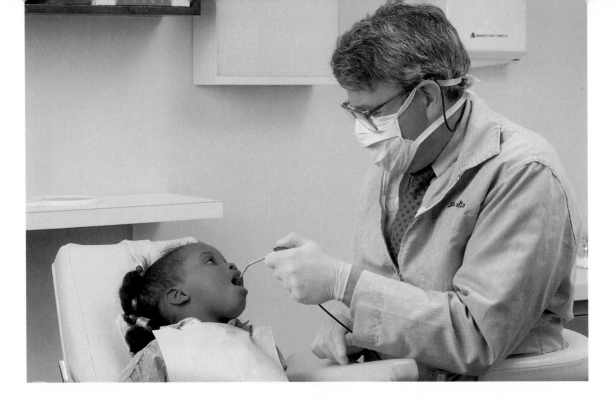

• a *syringe* that can squirt either water to wash your teeth or air to dry them off;

• a *suction tube* that keeps your mouth from filling up with water.

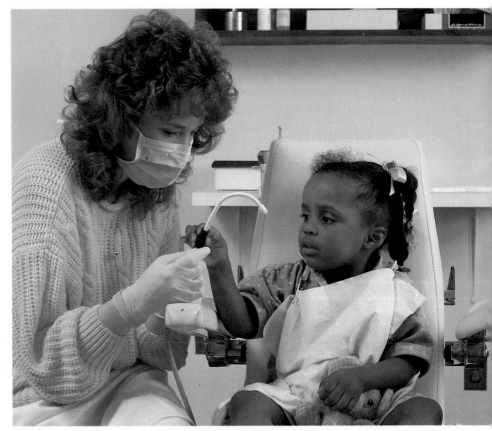

If you want to see what's going on, your dentist might let you hold another mirror so *you* can look into your mouth, too.

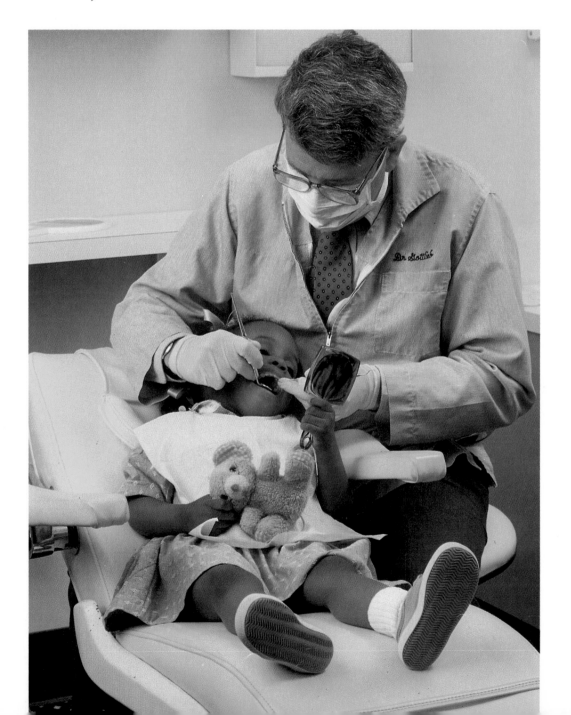

If you want to know what the dentist is going to do, it's okay to ask. Dentists understand that some people really like to know what's about to happen.

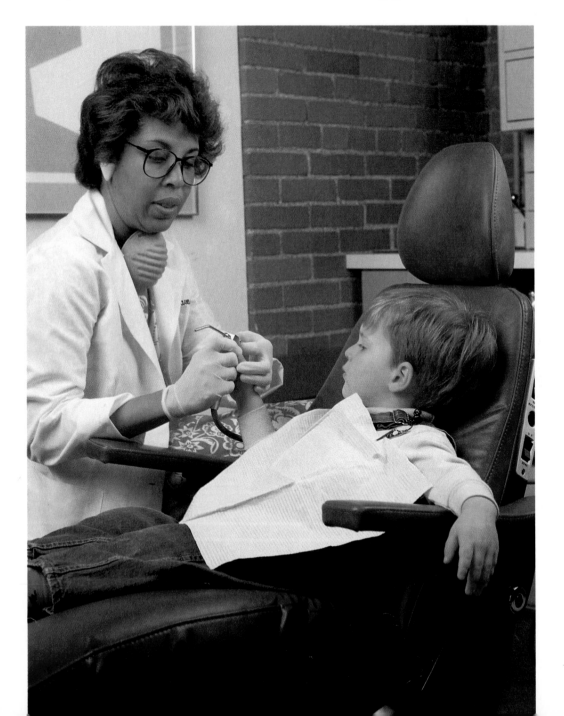

Your dentist may ask you to brush your teeth while you're there—and help you learn how to brush well. You might also rinse out your mouth with something that shows where your toothbrush didn't reach. The rinse turns those parts of your teeth red or yellow—but just for a little while.

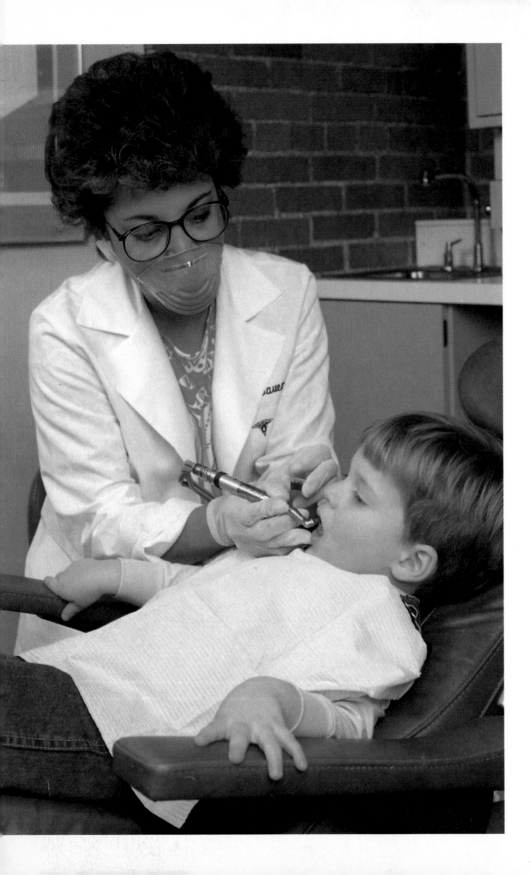

When dentists or their helpers clean people's teeth, they may use an electric cleaner with a rubber tip that spins and tickles a little. They usually use a special toothpaste, too.

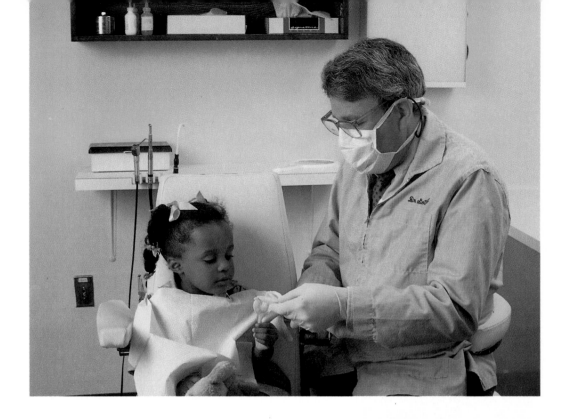

Your dentist may decide to use *fluoride* on your teeth. That's a kind of liquid that helps to make them stronger. Fluoride is good for your teeth, but it's not good for your stomach. That's why dentists tell people not to swallow it.

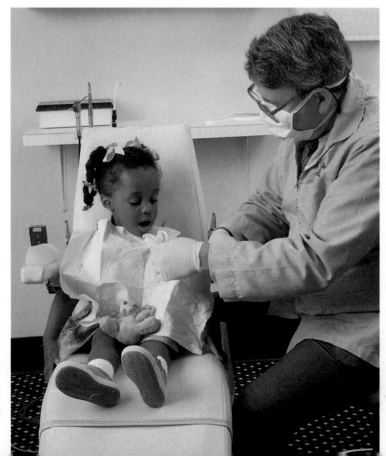

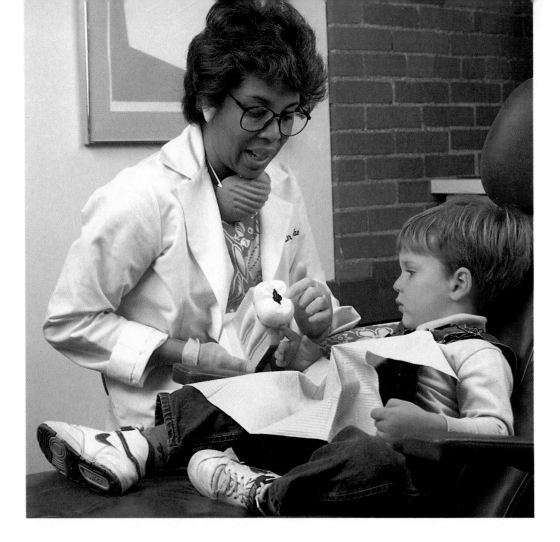

Dentists like to show and tell people important things about their teeth. Even when people take good care, their teeth can sometimes get soft spots called *caries* . . . many people call them *cavities.* Dentists need to clean out these soft spots and fill them with something hard that will help make the teeth strong again. Dentists don't usually do that on a person's first visit, but if you ever have a cavity in a tooth, you can be sure that your dentist will know the best way to fill it.

Dentists can tell you ways to take good care of your teeth at home—to keep them clean and healthy. For instance, brushing carefully in the morning and especially at bedtime, or after meals, is an important part of tooth care. It can be hard to hold a toothbrush and make it reach all around in front and in back of your teeth. Your mom or dad will need to help you for a while.

No matter what you do, a toothbrush can't get into the tight places between your teeth and keep those places clean. That's why people need to use *dental floss* as well as a toothbrush. Using floss takes practice, and while you're learning you'll also need help with that.

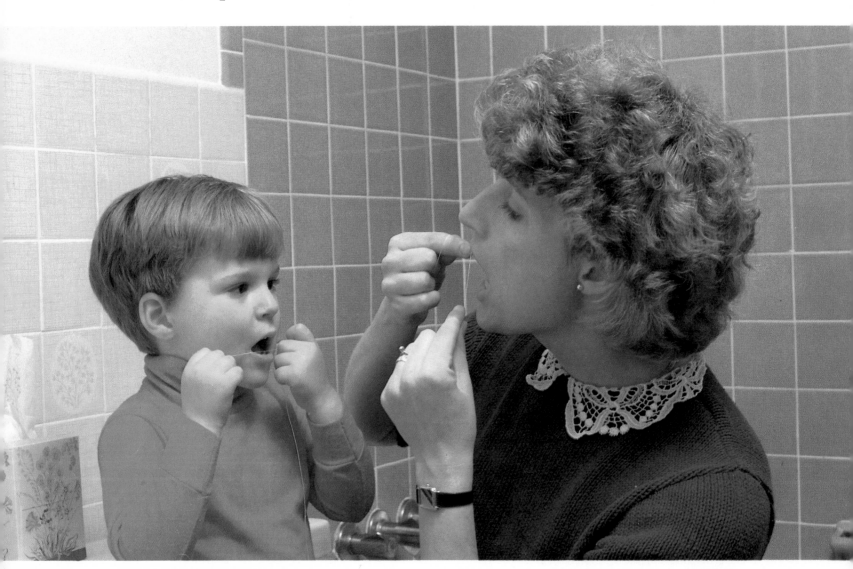

What you eat makes a lot of difference in keeping your teeth healthy. Some foods like milk and fruits and vegetables help make your teeth strong. But other foods, like things with lots of sugar in them, can be bad for your teeth. That's why the people who care for you don't want you to eat too many sweet things.

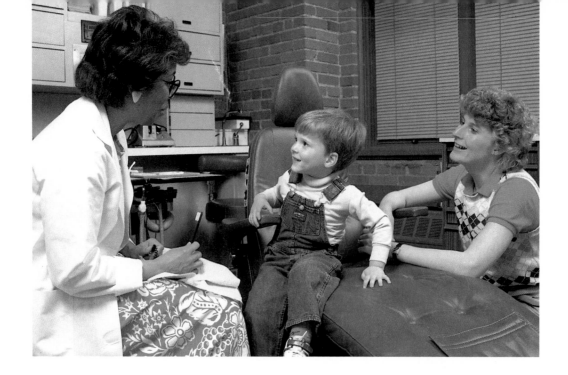

It's not always easy to take good care of ourselves, so it can be a really good feeling to know that there are people like mothers and fathers and dentists and their helpers who care about how we're growing . . . and who are there to give us all the help we need!

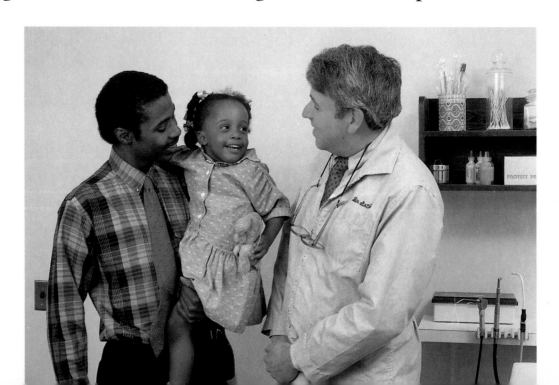